RISEN!

The First 40 Days
of Your Christian Life

C. Philip Slate

Risen! The First 40 Days of Your Christian Life
© 2016 by DeWard Publishing Company, Ltd.
P.O. Box 6259, Chillicothe, Ohio 45601
800.300.9778
www.deward.com

Cover design by Eric Wallace.

The preponderance of Bible quotations are taken from the The Holy Bible, English Standard Version®, copyright © 2001 by Crossway Bibles, a publishing ministry of Good News Publishers. Used by permission. All rights reserved. Any emphasis in Bible quotations is added.

Reasonable care has been taken to trace original sources for any excerpts and quotations appearing in this book and to document such information. For material not in the public domain, fair use standards and practices were followed. Should any attribution be found to be incorrect or incomplete, the publisher welcomes written documentation supporting correction for subsequent printing.

Printed in the United States of America.

ISBN: 978-1-936341-89-4

Introduction

After Jesus was baptized (read Matt 3.13–17) He was led by the Spirit of God into a deserted area where He was to be tempted by the devil. He fasted forty days and forty nights and then the devil tempted Him three times (read Matt 4.1–11). Often Satan does not cause people a lot of trouble as long as they remain non-Christians or become shallow, "lukewarm" believers. When they obey the Lord, however, and declare a serious new allegiance, a commitment to follow Jesus, Satan will often cause them real problems. For that reason the following forty spiritual activities are provided for you, one for each of the next forty days, beginning today. They are intended to bless you during the first forty days after your baptism.

When you were baptized you identified yourself with the death, burial, and resurrection of Jesus. You "died" to the practice of sin when you repented, made up your mind to live for God. You showed confidence in the death of Jesus when you were "buried" with Him in baptism. Then you were identified with Him in His resurrection when you, too, were raised up. In baptism you were "raised up to walk in newness of life." Risen! You are a new creature embarking on a new journey. The activities for the next forty days are to get you started on that wonderful journey. (See the end of this booklet for a fuller explanation of your death, burial, and resurrection.)

In these little daily exercises you will often be directed to read Scripture and at times be challenged to memorize a few choice verses that will help you. _Read every verse of all biblical references._ The writer of Psalm 119 wrote that God's word "is a lamp to my feet and a light to my pathway" (v 105). Notice how verse 11 of that chapter reads: "I have hidden your word in my heart that I might not sin against you." Along with prayer and encouragement from fellow Christians, having God's Word in your heart and mind provides both guidance and protection. Notice that Jesus quoted Scripture each time He resisted the devil's temptations (Matt 4.4, 7, 10). The written Word of God will be a great help to you in knowing how God wants you to live, encouraging you to live that way, and helping to protect you from sin and big mistakes. In the following exercises, look up every biblical reference given in the text. Take your time as you work through each daily section. They are all short. Occasionally, you might want even to review some of the sections to fix them in your mind.

Most of these sections are brief considerations of much larger subjects. Imagine a visitor from another country who knows nothing about baseball, basketball, American football, or golf. It is possible, of course, in three or four paragraphs to explain to that visitor the main goals and purposes of each of those sports. Those short descriptions may be accurate as far as they go, but full-size books have been written about each of them because each sport has a lot of details and variables. It is somewhat that way with the subjects in this booklet. People have written entire books on prayer, God, Jesus, the Holy Spirit, heaven, hope, temptation, judgment, and so on. The following daily readings, however, will serve as valuable introductions to the larger subjects.

A story has been handed down about a wealthy man who approached the famous educator Mark Hopkins (1802–1887), then President of Williams College, wanting to pay for his son to get his college degree more quickly than others. "I can pay for it," he said confidently. It is reported that Mr. Hopkins responded, "Well, Sir, it depends on what you want your son to be. When the Lord God wants an oak tree he takes a hundred years to produce it; when he wants a squash he takes three months!" Well said. Similarly, we become seasoned, mature, and deeply admired Christians over a period of time. We humans can be pretty stubborn when it comes to being molded into what God wants of us. After all, if we could master the Christian faith in three months it wouldn't be very valuable, would it?

The Christian faith is much like what Gregory the Great said of the Bible: "It is a book like a stream in which both the lamb may wade and the elephant may swim." New Christians can enjoy their new life; older Christians are still challenged by it.

Ideally, you should go through these daily sections at the same time you are in a class for new Christians or have a mentor with whom you can talk as you go along. I hope this can be arranged for you.

So, let us begin today, the first full day of your new life in Christ, and move on from there.

DAY 1
Rejoice!

Since you have responded to what God has directed you to do to become a Christian—to trust Him and His Son, Jesus—you can be *assured* that you are a Christian, a child of God. All of your past sins have been forgiven (Acts 2.38), blotted out (Acts 3.19), and from now on God will never hold those sins against you (Heb 8.12). In other words, you will never have to answer to God for those wrongs. Your soul has been purified (1 Pet 1.22). How wonderful!

You don't deserve any of that—none of us does. We have those blessings through God's kindness when we trust and obey Jesus, God's Son whom He sent into the world as Savior. That is what God's *grace* means: He shows kindness and goodness to us that we don't deserve.

Long before you and I were born God did great things for us. He was very patient with people who sinned and walked in their own foolish ways as though He did not even exist. In spite of that, God loved people (John 3.16). He sent Jesus into the world to live a sinless life, to show us how to live, to give wonderful guidance, and eventually to be a "sin offering" for us. In other words, God was willing to put our sins on Jesus, who did no sin (2 Cor 5.21; 1 Pet 2.24). You were bought with a price (the death of Jesus) and thus are not your own (1 Cor 6.19–20). These are only a few of the blessings you received. In time you will learn many more.

Now, before you go to sleep tonight, or at some point today, voice a prayer (even out loud) in which you pray something like this: "Dear God, I want to thank You for forgiving my sins and accepting me as Your own. I don't deserve this, so all I can do now is to thank You sincerely and to promise that I will do my best to live the way You want me to live. In the name of Jesus I pray. Amen"

Note: The little word "Amen" in a prayer context means, "let it be so" *or to express approval or agreement.*

DAY 2

ABCs

Yesterday—or whenever you became a Christian—was a big day in your life. You began a new path of life. At that moment you did not—you could not—realize how significant that step was. It is like a child's learning the alphabet, the ABCs. Little do children know that with those letters they will eventually be able to make words, then sentences, then paragraphs as they write letters, articles, or perhaps even books. They don't know that every time they use a dictionary they will benefit from learning the ABCs in order. That is the way it is in becoming a Christian. Much exciting growth and development are ahead for you. At this point you can hardly realize how different and meaningful your future will be as a child of God, or a Jesus-follower. It is also like climbing a rather tall hill or mountain. Halfway up you may pause to get your breath, but already you want to say, "Wow! Look at that view." So you go on to the top, feeling the effort involved in the climb will be rewarded by the view and the memory of it. That is why God wants us to stick with our commitment and not to give up or fall back. One of Jesus' apostles, Paul, went back to the young churches he had started and encouraged them to "remain true to the faith" (Acts 14.22). He charged others to "be steadfast, unmovable" (1 Cor 15.58).

Now, at some point during this second day of your Christian life, again pray to God—this should be a daily thing for you—thanking Him for the blessings he gives you. This time you also should ask Him to give you help as you begin your growth. Pray something like this. "My Father in heaven, I thank You for giving me life, breath and all things. You sustain me daily. On this second day of my commitment to you, O Lord, I ask You to give me strength to carry out my pledge to be loyal to You. Help me to lean on my brothers and sisters in Christ so they can help me. I want to be Your servant. In Jesus' name I pray. Amen." In time you will begin to voice your own concerns and requests to God.

Assignment: Memorize a short verse: Psalm 119.105. Remember the location of the verse, the book, chapter, and verse. Get someone to help you find an up-to-date standard translation of the Bible.

DAY 3
A Baby

There is nothing wrong with being a baby. Usually, parents rejoice when babies are born. But a person can be an adult in one way and yet a baby in other ways. I was a strong and robust 24-year-old man when I began to learn the Hebrew language, but my teacher used a Jewish children's book to teach us the alphabet with large Hebrew letters. I was full-grown in one way but a baby in learning Hebrew. That is the way it is when we become Christians, regardless of our physical age. We begin as babies.

In London, England during the 1960s "Grandma" Sones, as we called her affectionately, became a Christian at age 75. She was born in the 19th century, had lived through two world wars, lost a son in the second, outlived an alcoholic husband, and raised a family. She had seen a lot of life, but as a Christian she was a baby at 75. Peter gave directions to such new Christians, "Like newborn babies, crave pure spiritual milk, so that by it you may grow up in your salvation, now that you have tasted that the Lord is good" (1 Pet 2.2). Becoming a "grown up" in the faith is a wonderful thing. Strive for it and allow sufficient time for it to grow. Many things that are valuable require time to develop.

Now, take the time to write down on a piece of paper why you decided to follow Jesus and be obedient to Him in baptism. Then put it in an envelope, address it to yourself, and seal it. Keep it. One day it will be useful to you. Now, just for the next week or so, write down any concerns, fears, or questions you have in this early part of your Christian life. No question is too simple to ask. Small misunderstandings at the beginning can cause problems later. So, ask questions. You can get help on them.

In your prayers today thank God for each meal you eat. Notice how Paul did that in the presence of pagan sailors on his way to Rome (Acts 27.35). Being thankful for food and other things is a way of acknowledging that we are dependent on God, the giver of every good and perfect gift (Jas 1.17). Make it a habit to be thankful.

Read: Ephesians 5.18–20 and Colossians 3.16.

DAY 4
The Lord's Supper (1)

Soon you will partake of the Lord's supper for the first or second time. This activity is a vital part of your Christian growth since it is a weekly reminder of the basis of your salvation and security: Jesus Christ's death, burial, and resurrection. Read Matthew 26.17–30. There are four accounts of the Lord's supper in the New Testament, and in the ones by Luke and Paul emphasis is placed on Jesus' statement, "do this in remembrance of me" (1 Cor 11.24–25). So, when you eat a piece of the bread, remember the sufferings Jesus endured in His *body*, for you; and as you drink the fruit of the vine remember the *blood* He shed in the giving up of life, for you. He, the only sinless One, did that for us as sinful people in order that we might be forgiven and become something else, something new. We never outgrow the need to recall the basis of our salvation and our hope. It keeps us focused.

When you remember the suffering Jesus, the gift of God's love, each Lord's day (Sunday) over many years you will gain strength and stability. It is similar to our eating food daily so that over several years we grow from small children to full grown men and women. It is the accumulated effects of regular eating that enables us to grow, both physically and spiritually. So, as you participate in the Lord's supper week by week read and meditate on an account of the crucifixion and resurrection of Jesus. Read one of the songs or hymns about the Lord's supper.

As you will learn shortly, there is much more to the Lord's supper than memory, though memory is very powerful in its effects. We will pay attention to several other dimensions of the Lord's supper, all designed to help the Jesus-follower to stay on track.

In prayer today you can usefully thank God again for His love for you in giving the gift of His Son, Jesus. *Use your own words in pledging or promising loyalty to Him.* We pray "in Jesus' name" because He is the only mediator between us and God, our heavenly Father (1 Tim 2.5).

DAY 5
The Lord's Supper (2)

When partaking of the Lord's supper, a Christian may engage in several mental and spiritual activities. Earlier, we noticed that "remembering" is one thing we can do, and memory is powerful. God gave the Jews several feasts and activities by which they were to remember what He had done for them in the past. Those memories were to produce thanksgiving and a determination to remain faithful to God because of His blessings. The Lord's supper, however, involves much more than memory.

Memory looks backward, but those who partake of the Lord's supper are also to look forward. Read 1 Corinthians 11.17–26. Note the closing phrase in verse 26: "until he comes." The Lord's supper *nourishes the hope* you have as a Christian. It is to remind you that you are on your way to something better that will take place at the final coming of Jesus. The Lord's supper points to the bright future we have through what Jesus did and can do for us. We need that weekly nourishment for our souls.

Another focus of the Lord's supper is *thanksgiving.* The fruit of the vine (the juice of the grape) is referred to as the "cup of blessing" (1 Cor 10.16), or the cup of thanksgiving. The word "eucharist," often used by the second-century church, is adapted from the Greek word that means "thanks" or "thanksgiving." Weekly communion is a profound time for thanksgiving to God for the great blessings He gives us in Christ. This part of the Lord's supper should be associated with joy and praise.

A final emphasis on the supper in this lesson is "*proclamation*" or speaking a message (see 1 Cor 11.26). When we participate in the supper we "proclaim" or "show forth" the significance of the Lord's death until He comes. It is a way of saying to others, "I believe that the death and resurrection of Jesus are critically important, and I am basing my life on what Jesus did for me in those actions."

Eating bread and the fruit of the vine does not work magic in your soul. *The values of the Lord's supper lie in your motives and intentions, your purposes and thoughts.* As one hymn writer put it, "And so our feeble love is fed, until he comes." This is one reason we do it every week.

DAY 6
The Bible in English

The Old Testament was originally written in Hebrew with a few sections in Aramaic, a first cousin to Hebrew, while the New Testament was originally written in common, everyday Greek. Unless we can read those languages we need someone to *translate* the Bible into our language. Happily, we are very blessed to have Bibles that are translated into English. A number of people were killed for making some of the early translations into English. But thanks to them and others, we have the wonderful word of God in our hands in a language we can understand. Read Psalm 19.7–11.

One translation renders James 1.21 like this: "Therefore, get rid of all moral filth and the evil that is so prevalent, and humbly accept the word planted in you, which can save you" (New International Version). Make it your practice each day to spend at least a little time reading "Scripture" (that is what it is often called in the New Testament). God will bless you through His Word. It is the "living and powerful" word (Heb 4.12).

The Bible is not God; it is the word of God. It reveals much about God and His way for us humans, but it also points to Him as the object of our love and devotion, our worship and allegiance. We sing about this in one of our hymns: "Beyond the sacred page we seek Thee, Lord." Apart from Scripture there is no reliable information about God and His will for us humans. We do not discover God by our efforts. He has revealed Himself in many ways over many years (Heb 1.1–2). Those messages were written down for all to read. That is the Bible, Scripture.

When we get away from Scripture we do not know where we are going spiritually. We will be at the mercy of our age, a culture that has lost its way.

In your prayers today be sure to thank God for revealing Himself and His way to us, and for making it possible through His servants for us to have Scripture in our own language.

DAY 7

Congregation

Someone wrote, "The strength of the wolf is in the pack; the strength of the pack is in the wolf." Like wolves, Christians are to develop strength and integrity as individuals, but they will also find some of their strength in the congregation, the local church, of which they are a part. In Western civilization we place much emphasis on the individual with his or her rights and freedoms. That is not all bad, but it tends to neglect emphasis on human responsibility in and to groups. As humans we develop in relationships with other humans. A German proverb runs, "A man [alone] is no man." People become really human through relationships with other humans. We are meant to be connected.

The idea of an isolated, free-floating Christian is not a part of New Testament teaching because it is not the will of God. "Iron sharpens iron, and one man sharpens another" (Prov 27.17). Accordingly, most mature Christians will point to several fellow-Christians who inspired, taught, or modeled the Christian life for them. Charcoal burns when it is in a heap, but the isolated piece goes out. So does the independent, isolated Christian.

The Christians to whom the book of Hebrews was written were being persecuted (Heb 12.4, 12–13). As one means of surviving and keeping their faith they were urged not to stop their "meeting together" (10.23–25) since that was a major place where they were to give and receive encouragement to continue in their faith.

So important were those group meetings that the earliest Christians "*devoted themselves*" to "the apostles' teaching and fellowship, to the breaking of bread and the prayers" (Acts 2.42). They were together often, "breaking bread in their homes" (v 46). It is still very important to gather when the church gathers, and even to meet in small groups with fellow Christians for conversation, prayer, and encouragement.

In your prayer today, ask God to direct you to a few fellow Christians who will "sharpen" you and give you encouragement to survive and grow in Christ.

DAY 8

Christian Service

Usually when people become Christians they feel indebted to God. They want to do something in order to say, "Thank You for what You have done for me!" But how do we do that? We can never repay God for what He has done for us. If we could repay Him then we would *earn* our salvation. That is impossible, however, since our salvation and hope are much too valuable for us to earn. We are saved by God's kindness, His grace (Eph 2.8–9). So, how can we respond to God's kindness to us?

Obviously, prayer is one way to express thanks to God. We are always to be thankful (Col 3.15; 1 Thes 5.17).

Another thing we can do is to render Christian service. Jesus set the agenda early in his ministry when He said He did not come to be served, but to serve (Mark 10.43–45). He showed compassion on people (Mark 6.34). He engaged in evangelizing (telling good news), teaching and instructing, and doing compassionate service (Matt 4.23). These three actions are what we see in the earliest church as described in the book of Acts and in the Epistles (letters). These are actions for both the individual disciple and the local church. Read Galatians 6.9–10.

It is important early is your Christian life to find something you can do for God, some form of Christian service. We are God's workmanship, "created in Christ Jesus *for good works*" (Eph 2.10). Talk to a respected person about this. Find a widow down the street that needs her yard mowed or her house cleaned. Visit someone in the hospital to give her or him encouragement and let them know you care. Give some of your money to a worthy cause. Tell someone you are glad you became a Christian. Thank a teacher or preacher for what you think is a good lesson. Offer to help around the church building. Comfort a hurting friend. Write notes of thanks or encouragement. You get the idea. Each person has something she or he can do for God. Be creative.

When you have opportunities, attend a class or read a book that is designed to teach you how to do various ministries, like teaching a class or speaking to others about our wonderful Savior, Jesus.

DAY 9

Think Like a Christian

You have now been a Christian, a disciple of Jesus, for a week or more. Good for you! The way new Christians become strong and mature is a day at a time, a week at a time, a year at a time. But one danger is "plateauing," reaching a certain level and then settling for that. That is very dangerous. That cheats you and disappoints God. It isn't merely a matter of learning more facts about the Bible, valuable as that is. It goes beyond that to developing greater Christian character, developing the ability to think like a Christian, and living like a disciple of Jesus.

A hundred years or so ago there was a minor revival in the study of philosophy in the USA. A practical, down-to-earth man said, "I don't see any point in studying philosophy because that won't butter your bread." Someone replied, "No, but it has a way of helping you to enjoy your bread when you have no butter to put on it." He was referring to *perspective*. Everyone who lives, including Christians, will have setbacks and disappointments. Jesus did. How are Christians to view that? The way we think about those things, the way we react to them, is a product of our perspective on our world. Sometimes it is referred to as our "world-view." There are biblical ways of viewing pain and suffering, of illness and good health, of wealth and poverty—the totality of life. The Old Testament books of Job,

Habakkuk, and many Psalms provide perspectives on the disappointing events of life. Oddly enough, many people can handle poverty better than they can handle wealth. We all need the perspectives God gives us on the life we live.

Knowing and meditating on the Word of God (Psa 1.1–2), growing in prayer, being sharpened by fellow-Christians, and participating in several other Christian activities are the means of developing such perspectives.

In your prayers today, praise God; thank Him for His blessings, and ask Him to strengthen you in your quest to grow in Christ.

Memorize 1 Peter 2.2–3.

DAY 10
Farming on Diamond Mines!

George Henderson wrote about Mrs. Susana Goosen, a widow who lived on a small farm in South Africa, a plot of land on which she and her husband had eked out a meager living for many years. She died in poverty, having nothing but three goats and a bag of meal. However, that little farm lay over millions of dollars worth of diamonds that were eventually mined from it. The Goosens never knew the treasures that existed beneath the surface of their own property, just a few acres of land.

Regrettably, many people are that way about their Christian faith. They go through life at a very shallow level of understanding and spiritual development, often even drifting away from the One whom they embraced at one time as Savior and Lord of life. When that happens, a three-fold tragedy occurs. It is the ultimate tragedy to drift away from the Lord and eventually *be* lost. Second, it could have been prevented had the person chosen not to scratch out a "living" by functioning only on the surface. The third tragedy is that the person withheld from God the glory, praise, and worship He is due from the Christian's life.

Determine early in your Christian life that you will not spend your life merely scratching on the surface. Commit yourself to grow in Christ. Dig deeper. Doing that is a big part of these little lessons that you are reading and processing. Let them inform you, encourage you, and give you some of the guidance you will need.

No matter what your age, God takes you where you are and moves you on from there, providing you work with Him. He is "for you" (Rom 8.31). As you will see, He makes available to you many helps as a Christian that you never had before you decided to give yourself to Jesus Christ for forgiveness, acceptance, and re-formation of character. *Follow through with it, both for God's praise and for your enrichment in the life to which you have committed yourself.* Go beyond the milk goats; mine some of the diamonds.

DAY 11
Our Wonderful God

When the pagan people of Thessalonica became Christians, it was said that they "turned to God from idols to serve the living and true God" (1 Thes 1.9). There were then, as now, many false gods; "there are many 'gods' and 'lords'—but in reality there is one God, the Father, from whom are all things and from whom we exist ..." (1 Cor 8.6). In our society "false gods," idols, may be success, status, possessions—anything that claims our highest allegiance. But what is the true God like? Is He near or far away?

From the first book of the Bible (Gen 1.1) to the last (Rev 4.8–11; 14.7), God is presented as the Creator of heaven and earth and its contents. God as Creator is one of the great teachings of Scripture. Read what Paul said about God in a sermon to pagans in Athens, Greece (Acts 17.22–31). God created in the past, but He continues to "uphold all things by the word of his power" (Heb 1.3). He sustains his creation; He "gives to all mankind life and breath and everything" (Acts 17.25). He makes the sun and rain to come on good and evil people (Matt 5.45). He does not need us since He is self-sufficient (Psa 50.9–11), but we need Him!

When God made humans He made them more than visible bodies. He made humans in His image, after His likeness (Gen 1.26–27). We have a spiritual dimension, and because of that we are capable of knowing and loving God. He made us for Himself and He wants to bestow His love on us. Note the description God gives of Himself (Exod 34.5–7). That statement, in part or whole, is repeated several times in Scripture. Note that He is a God of both love and justice. He is said to be both love (but love is not God!) and a consuming fire (Heb 12.28–29). He is "just" (fair, equitable) (Dan 4.37; 1 John 1.9). God is not an angry Power who is out to get us

This is the God to whom we pray, the God we worship. He is powerful enough to hear us and act. He wants our loyalty and allegiance so He can pour his love on us and make us partakers of (sharers in) His nature (2 Pet 1.4). As time passes you will learn more about our wonderful God. He is the center of everything.

DAY 12
Temptation

After a person becomes a Jesus-follower it is common to feel the pull of the old way of life. You may find yourself tempted to return to some of your old ungodly habits and values of life. That is the devil's effort to get you back in his camp. What is a Christian to do about those temptations?

It is not a sin to be tempted. We know that because Jesus himself was tempted (Matt 4.1ff) and yet never sinned (Heb 4.14–15). God never tempts a person to do evil (Jas 1.13). Rather, when we are tempted "God is faithful, and he will not let you be tempted beyond your ability, but with the temptation he will also provide the way of escape, that you may be able to endure it" (1 Cor 10.13). So, when you are tempted, always look for that way of escape, the help God provides.

According to James 1.12–15, this is the way temptation works. We are tempted when lured and enticed by our own desires. But sin does not occur until the desire expresses itself or is put into actions. If that sin is not checked and dealt with, the sin brings forth death. If we do sin, then God has provided us an Advocate. Read 1 John 2.1–2.

At times sins of long standing are hard to overcome. The temptation continues to arise. In those cases you should be doubly prayerful about them, and should seek out a Christian you have come to trust. Confess the difficulty you are having (James 5.16), name it to that helper so he or she can pray for you and encourage you. Addictions are harder to handle, but there are specific Christian groups that can help you to overcome even problems with drugs, alcohol and other addictions you may have. You can overcome them with God's help, and a part of the help He provides is your select Christian friends.

Memorize the following clauses from two verses in James 4.7–8: "Resist the devil, and he will flee from you" and "Draw near to God, and he will draw near to you." Aren't those two statements wonderful? Focusing on our positive efforts to develop godliness will go a long way toward handling temptations. *Read also 1 Peter 5.8–9.*

DAY 13
New Life

One of the priceless blessings a Jesus-follower enjoys is that she or he has begun a new kind of life with new and better focuses. In a long passage (John 10.1–18) where Jesus teaches about His being the good shepherd, He said, "I came that they may have life and have it abundantly" (v 10). Jesus was referring to a different kind of life, a different quality of life, not more of the same old life we had before becoming His follower.

This "abundant life" is at times referred to as "eternal life," in this case not because it lasts eternally (though that is true), but because it comes from the realm of eternity. Jesus prayed, "This is eternal life, that they know you the only true God, and Jesus Christ whom you have sent" (John 17.3). As you will learn, "knowing God" is not merely knowing about God, but knowing God through prayer, meditation, living His kind of life, and so forth. It involves a relationship with God.

Doing things *because* you know God wants you to do them is a way of knowing God. In the movie *Chariots of Fire,* Scottish standout in the 1924 Olympics, Eric Liddle told his sister, "God made me for a purpose, and that purpose is to go to China. But He also made me fast, and when I run I feel His pleasure." Yes, knowing that you are living out the purpose God has for you gives you a sense of "feeling His pleasure." That is a part of knowing God.

Another way this idea is expressed is found in 2 Peter 1.3–5 (read) where it is referred to as "partaking of the divine nature." Telling the truth is God's nature, seeking the good of others (love) is God's nature, and helping the poor and needy is God's nature. That is one reason Christians are directed to "be imitators of God" (Eph 5.1). That is, follow God's nature as it is expressed in human relationships. Read Ephesians 5.1–21.

In your prayers today, be thankful to God for revealing to humans what "abundant life" and "partaking of the divine nature" are about. One reason pagans were attracted to the earliest Christians was that the Christians simply lived a superior life. They had a higher quality of life than the pagans. That attraction still works today.

DAY 14
Quiet Time

In the midst of his busy work of preaching, teaching, and healing, Jesus took time to get away and pray. On one occasion, early in the morning, while it was still dark, Jesus went out to a quiet, deserted place to pray (read **Mark 1.35–39**). Later, after Jesus' twelve apostles returned from their "trial run" of doing what Jesus had trained them to do, they gathered around Jesus and reported on their work. Jesus said to them, "Come away by yourselves to a desolate place and rest a while." Mark added, "for many were coming and going, and they had no leisure even to eat." So they took a boat to a desolate place to be by themselves (Mark 6.30–32).

Mature Christians have long known the need to have *quiet times* for meditation and prayer. While disciples of Jesus are supposed to be among people as salt and light to serve and influence them for good, they can become tired; they need to escape the distractions and business of life so they can focus on God and his Word to mankind. Good things happen when believers are alone with God—no pretense, no put-on—just the individual in meditation, reading, and praying. It might even be a time when you discover some deep spiritual need in your own life. By identifying it you can more easily deal with it.

You will be wise to create such times to be alone with God.

For some, it is early in the morning, while for others it is the end of the day. Pick your time and use it for your growth. Write notes on your thoughts. Read the Psalms to get glimpses of the greatness and goodness of God. Remember, one is "blessed" (that is, in a happy, good position) who "meditates on the word of God" (Psa 1.2). God will bless you for meditating on His Word and His ways, and on who He is.

Additionally, there are a number of good devotional books you may read in your quiet time. A mature Christian can point you to some of them. It is also a good time to memorize a verse to have in your heart (Psa 119.11).

DAY 15
Being at Peace with God

Because of what God did for us through Jesus Christ, and because you have yielded yourself to God in the manner specified in Scripture, you now have "peace with God" (Rom 5.1–2). How can any of us place a value on being at peace with the Maker of the universe? It is wonderful to go to sleep at night with confidence that you are at peace with God.

We have peace with God chiefly because He took the initiative to woo us away from sin and to Himself. That was and is the beginning of your journey with God. Sin separates us from God (Isa 59.1–2); it alienates us from God and makes us His enemies (Col 1.21). But through Jesus Christ, who bore our sins in His body on the cross, we are reconciled to God (Rom 5.10). The word "reconciled" means to become friends again. A man and his wife, or two friends, may have disputes and be separated, but when they are reconciled, they have come to terms with each other and renew their determination to live at peace. In our case, God took the initiative to bring us back so we can be at peace with Him. This involves so many blessings that they cannot be listed here, but several of them will be mentioned later in this little booklet. Carry on with the readings and activities day by day and you will be richly blessed.

Living at peace with God gives personal stability and establishes the basis upon which you can grow more and more pleasing to Him and be more personally fulfilled. He made us for that. Long ago Augustine of Hippo prayed, "O Lord, you have made us for yourself and we cannot rest in peace until we rest in you." Indeed.

The Bible, Scripture, is not about our search for God, though people do seek God. Rather, the story-line of Scripture is chiefly about God's seeking His wayward, arrogant human creatures who have lived at a distance from Him.

Briefly pray: "O God, my Creator and Sustainer, I praise

You and I thank You for revealing who You are and how I can be at peace with You. In Jesus' name. Amen."

DAY 16
Singing (1)

By now you have attended two or more assemblies, or meetings of Christians. You noticed that they sang songs. Why do disciples of Jesus do that? Oh, we know, don't we, that people like to sing and hear singing? We sing national anthems, love songs, and children's songs. We like music. It is universal. But, as many other activities and things, Christians have distinctive views on items like money, marriage, work, time and friends. It is, as noted earlier, their world-view.

You notice that they only sang in the assembly. There was no orchestra, guitar, violin, or organ. They just sang. In the Old Testament one notices that, especially in the temple, many instruments were used, and at times only instruments. But Jesus brought a higher level of worship and relationship with God. So, throughout the New Testament we observe Christians only singing. Everywhere the focus is on the meanings of the words, the sentiments expressed in those hymns. No emphasis is placed on the musical part of songs. Indeed, this singing-only position was so common and well known in the early centuries of the church that singing without instruments was called a cappella music. Those words did not mean "without instruments" but rather "after the manner of the church." This practice of the earliest church is written clearly in history. Singing was not an art form but a serious means of expressing ideas of praise to God and teaching each other. The musical part was important for memory and emotional qualities, but it was all functional and spiritual.

Through the centuries, Christian songs and hymns have nurtured people's souls. Meaningful hymns have been written in times of distress, persecution, and sorrow, as well as in times of rejoicing and thanksgiving. You will do well to learn to use these hymns meaningfully. In tomorrow's reading you will learn more about this practice.

Meanwhile, pay attention to the words of hymns. *Open a hymn book and read the words to pick up the meaning.* The musical notations are but a little boat to carry along the words.

DAY 17
Singing (2)

Following yesterday's reading, let us focus again on singing. Read now Ephesians 5.18–20 and Colossians 3.16–

17. Notice that some songs are to be sung "to one another." That expression implies that individuals are not singing alone in an assembly. Rather, they are together, and they sing songs that teach and encourage one another—songs like "Love One Another," "'Tis So Sweet to Trust in Jesus," and "A Mighty Fortress is Our God." On the other hand, some songs are to be sung to God as praise or prayer—like "Praise God from Whom All Blessings Flow," "Be With Me, Lord," and "Holy, Holy, Holy."

Several men have said, in one way or another, "I don't care who writes your theologies as long as I can write your hymns." Christian songs and hymns have a way of nurturing us. Whether in sorrow or happiness, people sing. When Paul and Silas were in the inner prison in Philippi it is not recorded that they talked deep theology or philosophy, nor even that they bemoaned their situation. Rather, at midnight they were "praying and singing hymns to God" (Acts 16.25). Did you notice that singing familiar hymns to God lay side-by-side with praying to God? When people write good songs and hymns they give us words that are useful to us. (Unfortunately, not all songs and hymns are good. Hymn writers can, and have, set to music ideas that are unhelpful, foolish, or even outright wrong.) That is why we need to sing good hymns, understand the words, and mean them when we sing. Otherwise we would be singing "in vain" (for nothing, emptily). Mean what you sing and the singing will mean more to you. When you don't understand the words and sentiments, don't sing them. God does not give us credit for merely singing tunes. Even in the Old Testament period, God disdained the empty songs of Israel since they were not serving him (Amos 5.23–4; 6.5).

When discussing their growth, many mature Christians will usually identify the singing of certain hymns as one important contribution to their development in Christ. Singing them fixes words in our minds. This is an important subject and an important part of your development in Christ. Pay attention to it.

DAY 18
Holy Spirit

A person has a lot of helps after becoming a Christian that she or he did not have before becoming a Christian. Among those helps is that of the Holy Spirit of God. Scripture is clear that the Holy Spirit is a gift that comes to those who surrender to God and become his children. Read Acts 2.38 and Galatians 4.6. Even the weak Christians at Corinth were told that the Holy Spirit was in their bodies, and that it was "from God" (1 Cor 6.19–20). For that reason they were told to "glorify God in their bodies." That is true for you and me as well.

The indwelling Spirit serves several purposes. He provides an encouragement to holiness, as noted in 1 Corinthians 6.20. If God honors your body enough to put His Spirit in it, you should not use it for unholy purposes. Further, the gift of the Spirit is a seal, a mark of identification that God has placed there to say to the unseen (by us) spirit world, "He is mine" or "She is mine" (2 Cor 1.22; Eph 1.14; 3.10). The Spirit also gives us strength and encouragement to bear the right kind of fruit in our lives. Read Galatians 5.16–26. The Spirit does not force us to be godly. It is possible to resist the Spirit (Acts 7.51), to go against his silent urging to act rightly. When one has a humble, submissive attitude toward God, however, He will provide help to live righteously and joyfully.

Scripture contains a vast amount of information about the Holy Spirit. In time you will learn more about the wonderful work of God's Holy Spirit in your life. But at this point you should just be assured that in the larger universe God has placed His mark on you and declared you to be his own. Determine to use your body for holy purposes, not evil ones, since God regards your body highly enough to place His Spirit in it.

Today thank God for giving you His Spirit. You don't understand it all, but you can benefit from it nonetheless. Long before we were told about the digestion process in our bodies, we ate and benefited from our food! God does things like that.

DAY 19
Review

If you are still keeping up with these daily readings and exercises, good for you. When you have the time, you will do well to review some of them. In fact, reviewing is an important activity. Why not review what happened when you first became a Christian not very long ago?

To do this, please turn now to Romans 5 where Paul was reviewing for the church at Rome what Jesus Christ had done for them. Read verses 1–11, but the heart of concern here is in vs. 6–11. Note that before yielding to God, you, like the Romans, were too "weak" to live rightly; you were "ungodly" (v 6), a "sinner" (v 8) and an "enemy" to God (v 10). While [people were] still in that condition Christ died for the ungodly (vv 6, 8, 10) and shed his blood for sinners (v 9). As a result of what Christ earned for us, and because we trusted him as he directed, we are now "justified" (put in a position of "not guilty") and "saved" (from the guilt and punishment of our sins) (v 9), "reconciled" (made a friend to God) (v 10), and put in a position where we may "rejoice" in God (v 11). How wonderful! Rejoice!

When you began your walk as a disciple you came to believe that Jesus was the trustworthy Son of God, you repented (decided to turn your back on your own way of life, a sinful life) and turned yourself toward Christ. Finally, you were baptized into a relationship with the Father,

Son, and Holy Spirit (Matt 28.19). You were buried in and resurrected from water, thus identifying your self with Jesus in His saving actions: death, burial, and resurrection (1 Cor 15.1–4). You were not trying to earn anything; you were raised "with him through faith in the powerful working of God" (Col 2.12). God works in our baptism! There we become identified with Jesus Christ. How incredibly wonderful that is!

That day and those actions nearly three weeks ago will be important for you the rest of your life since they form your spiritual foundation. We build on foundations, higher and higher.

DAY 20

You are a Person of Becoming

There is a strong human tendency to blame other people or circumstances for what we are, and especially our attitudes, desires, and weaknesses. People tend to blame their forefathers (their biological background) or their environment (their peers, neighborhoods, schools, brothers and sisters, and so forth) for their sins, shortcomings, and limitations. It is a way of saying, "I can't help it if I am this way; it is just the way I am." Often that attitude results in people's settling for what they are at the moment and making little or no effort to do better (or worse).

One way to know this is a wrong view of self is to look at history, at biographies of various people came from bad backgrounds with a lot of strikes against them and yet turned out to be quality, productive persons. On the other hand, some people who grew up with many advantages ended up as miserable characters who made no contributions to society, could not sustain a marriage, and were very unhappy persons. History argues against the view that we humans are "set in concrete" by our past. We can make choices.

That wrong view of self is also contrary to the way God made us. Adam and Eve were created sinless and placed in the garden of Eden, but they were creatures of choice; they could make decisions that had different outcomes (Genesis 3.1–19). John recorded that Jesus came to His own people, and to those who accepted Him He gave the "right to become" children of God (John 1.10–13). Yes, we humans are "beings of becoming"; we can and do change.

As sinners we turned and became Christians! Yes, it was clearly through God's initiative, His pulling, but we had to make a decision. As Christians we can make the wrong choice of trying to stay where we are, or we can yield to God and make choices by which we *become* more and more like God (Eph 5.1). We are capable of partaking more and more of the "divine nature," that way of life that comes from above. We are capable of greater Godlikeness.

*To grow in godliness, use that **becoming** feature of your nature as a human.*

DAY 21

The Christian's Sins

One reason you gave yourself to Jesus Christ, and one benefit of doing so, was to be free from the guilt of all past sins—to be forgiven and have those sins blotted from your record. What a joyous blessing that is. But as a new Christian you will soon learn, if you have not already, that you were not made perfect in that process of forgiveness and becoming a Jesus-follower. So, what should you do about the sins you commit now?

Read 1 John 1.5–10. John was writing to followers of Jesus (2.1, 12–14), not to non-Christians. He wrote to help them avoid sin, but he assured them that if they did sin they had an "advocate" (something like a lawyer, a mediator for them) to the Father (2.1–2). That is reassuring. Now read chapter 1.5–10. Working in reverse through the paragraph you will note that when people say either that they have *no* sin or that they have *not* sinned they are severely denounced (vv 8, 10). On the other hand, if they (and we) will be honest about weaknesses and sins God is faithful and just to cleanse and forgive. God does that, not because sins are unimportant, but because we have a relationship with Jesus, our Savior. Note verse **7**, a powerful and reassuring text worth memorizing. "Walking in the light" does not mean perfection since we will still sin. Those words refer to our *general course of life* as a

Jesus-follower. That is the condition in which "the blood of his Son cleanses us from all sin." When we identify sins in our lives, name them, and confess them to the Lord, seeking to overcome them, that is the condition in which we are confident that "the sins of Christians" will be forgiven. What a wonderful reassurance!

Since any and all sins made it necessary for Jesus to die, we want to grow in such a way that we reduce sins in our lives. To sin is to "miss the mark" that God has for us. We are called to a higher life, the "eternal life" noted earlier. So, while we want to do our best for our Lord and Savior, He is full of grace and is willing to forgive us when we confess our wrongs and go to Him for repair. Make it a practice in your prayer life to confess your sins to God and ask His forgiveness.

DAY 22
Sanctification

Wow! That's a big word and perhaps not familiar to you. But it is important since Paul wrote to quite ordinary Christians, "For this is the will of God, your sanctification" (1 Thes 4.3). In the same chapter (v 7) the same word is translated "holiness." But what is holiness?

We properly think of God as being holy (Rev 4.8). In

fact, no person or thing is holy in the sense that God is holy (Rev 15.4). It is God's nature to be in a category all his own. All other holiness of people and things is relative to God's holiness.

In the Old Testament, the vessels that went into the tabernacle were said to be "holy" in that they had been devoted to God, set apart for His purposes (Num 16.38). The seventh day Sabbath was holy to the Lord (Lev 23.3). But God also said to the people of Israel, "You are to be holy to me because I, the Lord, am holy, and I have set you apart from the nations to be my own" (Lev 20.26). That makes it clear: they were called a holy people because they had been "set apart" for a holy God. "Holyfied" is not a good English word, but that is what "sanctified" means: set apart for or devoted to some task or position.

In the New Testament, the words holy and sanctified, holiness and sanctification, also have a moral quality; that is, in their behavior Christians are to live the kind of life expected of those who belong to God, who want to avoid being shaped by a worldly outlook and lifestyle. That is clear in the verses that follow 1 Thessalonians 4.3. It is also stated in 1 Corinthians. 6.19–20 that "You are not your own; you were bought with a price."

Living with the self-concept "I belong to God" provides a big driving force for right living. If I belong to Him, through both my surrender and His purchase, I will want to do His will in my life. We become a holy people through Christ (1 Cor 1.30) and then we are able to move into the kind of life that is more and more like God wants.

Today be thankful to God for making you His own.

DAY 23

Judgment to Come

How would you like to live in a world where it really makes no difference how a person lives except for human preferences? That would mean that whether one lives like Adolph Hitler or the apostle Paul, like Joseph Stalin or the best Christian you ever knew, would make no difference in the end.

Actually, that is not the case at all. Jesus said that when he comes in his glory, at the end of time on earth, "all the nations of the world will be gathered before him, and he will separate them from one another" on the basis of the way they have lived (Matt 25.31–46). In his sermon in the city of Athens, Paul declared that God will "judge the world in righteousness" (Acts 17.31). Before the Roman ruler Felix, Paul preached about "righteousness, self-control and the judgment to come" (Acts 24.25). People who keep on sinning, turning their backs on God, have only "a fearful expectation of judgment and of raging fire that will consume the enemies of God" (Heb 10.26–27). That passage continues by stating, "it is a dreadful thing to fall into the hands of the living God (v 31). Statements like these are found throughout the New Testament, coming from Jesus and his apostles whom he trained and commissioned to teach as he had taught them (Matt 28.20). In other words, physical death is not the end for humans.

These emphases do not mean that God wants to scare us into loyalty to Him. God wants us to love Him because He first loved us. How would a father feel about his son if he knew that the son did not like him at all—perhaps even hated him—but was obedient because he feared the consequences? No, a father wants his children's love and loyalty. One reason our salvation is so great is that it involves deliverance from the "fearful expectation of judgment." The judgment is a way of pointing out how terrible sin really is.

So, as loving children we should reject and disdain all sinfulness and focus rather on love and loyalty to our loving God.

DAY 24

Becoming Like Jesus

Models are helpful. What child has not tried to imitate a parent, teacher, star athlete, musician, a TV personality? Most successful teachers, musicians, scholars, and others will point to specific people who were good models for them. Jesus' servant, Paul, once wrote, "Be imitators of me, as I am of Christ" (1 Cor 11.1). Paul knew that his life would be imitated by others, so he pointed out that he was imitating Christ. Paul exhorted the young preacher, Timothy, to "set the believers an example in speech, in conduct, in love, in faith…" (1 Tim 4.12). Yes, most of us tend to be selectively imitators.

Peter pointed out how Jesus behaved when He was persecuted and stated that in doing so He left us an example, "that we should follow in his steps" (1 Pet 2.21). John put it another way: "whoever says he abides in him (Jesus) ought to walk in the same way in which he walked" (1 John 2.6). Over and over in the Gospels we read of Jesus' saying, "Follow me," not just "keep My teachings" or "pay attention to these principles," important as they are. This makes reading the Gospels important since they contain most of the information we have about Jesus' behavior, His life in a world of people. Begin with the Gospel of Mark. Read it a chapter at a time and pay attention to Jesus' behavior. Then eventually read the other Gospels. God will bless you in those readings.

Trying to be like our chosen models can be discouraging at first. A young golfer can be crushed by his or her inability to hit the ball like a professional. The same goes for beginning musicians and athletes. But in the case of Jesus' example, God supplies us with help to grow in that kind of life. We noted earlier that we have the help of the Holy Spirit. Our fellow Christians give us encouragement. Hymns and prayers are also helpful. In other words, God supplies help to those who commit themselves to follow His way. It just takes time for us to conquer some old ways of behaving and thinking and to replace them with God's way. Be persistent. Seek some good models.

Today, pray for your own growth. Pray for good models to be in your life.

DAY 25
Prayer

It is a tragic thing to have access to God, to know that He will hear us when we pray, and then have little or nothing to say to Him! Most people do not know how to pray. It is no wonder that one of Jesus' disciples said, "Lord, teach us to pray, just as John taught his disciples" (Luke 11.1). Jesus then gave them a model prayer (Matt 6.9–13). Jesus prayed much, so it is clear that Christians need to pray.

At this point it will be useful for you to think of prayer as having at least four easy-to-remember components since they spell the word "Acts."

Adoration (praise). At times we sing, "Father, we adore You." That means we praise God. For some reason translators of our English Bibles do not use the word "adore" very much, but the idea or concept is clearly there. In our prayers it is important to acknowledge God's greatness, His power and wisdom, His amazing grace, His goodness. Many useful praise, worship, and adoration words or terms can be found in the Psalms. Become familiar with them and use them.

Confession. It is spiritually healthy for us to confess our sins to God, as we noticed earlier (1 John 1.9). Indeed, confession is one of the conditions under which Christ's blood cleanses us.

Thanksgiving. Often Christians are urged to be thankful (Col 3.15; 1 Thes 5.18). Expressing thanks is a way of acknowledging that God is the Giver of every good gift (Jas 1.17). Consider how many blessings God has given you and then thank Him. At times we sing, "Count your many blessings; name them one by one." When you do that it is hard to find a stopping place.

Supplication (requests). In 1 Timothy 2.1 some translations have "supplications" while others have "requests." Look up that word in an English dictionary. Jesus taught us to "ask" (Matt 7.7). Generally we find it easy to ask God for blessings, and that is appropriate. We need to say in prayers, as in life, "if the Lord wills" (see Jas 4.13–16).

These four categories are not the only components of prayer, but they are all important and a good way to start your prayer life. Indeed, even seasoned, mature Christians may use the same categories. *Make little lists under each heading and then pray for those things when you pray privately to God. Pray regularly (1 Thes 5.17).* "Seven days without prayer makes one weak." You will grow closer to God by praying to Him "in the name of Jesus Christ."

DAY 26

Hope: This Life on Earth Is Not All There Is!

One dreadful thing about not being a Christian is that there is no ground for hope after earthly life (1 Cor 15.19). As Christians, we do not have hope merely because we are humans; we have it because we are "in Christ," because we are Jesus-followers. Anchors hold ships steady in troubled waters. The writer of the book of Hebrews stated that hope serves as "an anchor of the soul" (Heb 6.19), and that is likely one reason Paul prayed that Christians may come "to know the hope" to which God had called them (Eph 1.18). We are less likely to turn back from Christ if we really come to know what we have (and will have) as a result of following Him and being loyal to Him. Hope is one thing that produces martyrs rather than cowards.

Specifically, the Christian hope involves the solid expectation of resurrection from the dead (1 Thes 4.13–18) and life with God. Peter referred to it as a "living hope" that does not "perish, spoil, or fade" (1 Pet 1.3–4). Being with God in and for eternity is a staggering thought, but that is the Christian's hope. Paul referred to his death as departing and "being with Christ" (Phil 1.21).

At times we use the word "hope" to mean something like "wish" or "desire." But Christian hope is characterized by assurance and confidence. It is not a guessing game or just a pious wish. It is certain because it is based on what Christ has done for us, not on the perfection of our obedience to him or completely sinless life.

God made us humans for Himself, in His image, after His likeness (Gen 1.26–27). We are capable of partaking of the "divine nature" (2 Pet 1.4), the nature that comes from God. Growing in that nature equips us for life with Him in eternity. We cannot understand the depths of this promise, but there it is, the Christian's hope. Rejoice!

Today as you pray, be particularly thankful to God for the hope He gives you through Jesus Christ. People who are without hope give up, despair, and at times even commit suicide because they can see no way out. Hope is wonderful!

DAY 27

Members of God's Family

Sooner or later someone will ask you, "What church are you a member of?" That is a fair question, and as Christians we should be prepared to answer it fairly.

In the New Testament there are nearly 100 different (Greek) words used to describe the people who belong to God, who are disciples of Jesus: body, church, people of God, and so forth. Here the focus is on one of those terms: the church as a spiritual family, God's household (1 Tim 3.15). Every society has groups of which people are members, but the local church is a special kind of group.

When we become Christians, that very act makes us members of God's family, the church Jesus started (see Matt 16.15–20). In other words, in the New Testament we do not read of doing something to become a member of Christ's church other than becoming a Christian, a Jesus-follower. Within that church, the members are referred to as "brothers" and "sisters" with God as their/our Heavenly Father. Those words are not religious titles; they point to relationships that come about because we have become disciples of Jesus. Read Romans 16.1 and 2 Peter 3.15 for such uses. Many Jesus-followers are closer to brothers and sisters in the church than they are to their blood relatives who are not Christians! That is because we share a spiritual life at a very different level.

God's family is not and cannot be formed simply by the voluntary actions of people who want to join another group. Our Christian family is created by God through Jesus Christ. It is composed of people who have come to Christ as weak and sinful, trusting in him for forgiveness and acceptance, and obeying him in repentance and baptism. That made us "new creatures," or a "new creation" (2 Cor 5.17). The church is referred to as "God's workmanship" (Eph 2.10). Satan could not make a Christian if he wanted to do so, and he would not make one if he could. So, we are not in a man-made group or family; we are the family of God! We do not deserve that, but we can and should enjoy and benefit from it.

Be thankful to God for your Christian family. As time passes it will become nearer and dearer to you. You should be a good brother or sister in that family.

Don't forget to pray today.

DAY 28
Handling Persecution

When Jesus came into the world He declared that most everything was wrong and needed correcting in one way or another. When what he taught conflicted with what the Jewish authorities and teachers held to be the right way, it was understandable that they persecuted Him: they lied about Him, tried to catch Him in some error, plotted against Him, and eventually killed Him. If we follow in His steps it is likely that we will be persecuted in one way or another.

Christians suffer persecution at different levels. In some parts of the world people are killed because they follow Jesus. In other cases they may fail to get a job or be denied a promotion at their work. They may be jeered at or made the object of jokes. What are Christians to do when these things happen?

First, don't think it is odd that these things should happen to you, as though it were something strange. That is the point Peter made to the persecuted Christians in what is now north-central Turkey (1 Pet 4.12). Two of Jesus' nine "Beatitudes" praised those who would be persecuted because of righteousness (read Matt 5.10–12). Since Jesus and some of His followers were persecuted, you are in good company when you suffer because of Him today. Some people have too little faith to be persecuted! *Second,* knowing about it ahead of time can help you to prepare for persecution; note Jesus' instructions to His apostles for this very reason (John 16.1–4). *Third,* arm yourself for it in advance. Plan how you will respond. Read 1 Peter 3.8–16; 4.7–8, 12–17. Peter pointed to the example of Jesus when He was persecuted (1 Pet 2.21–24).

In time you will learn from both Scripture and other Christians how to respond to different types of persecution. Those times can be emotionally hard, but they can be wonderful times to demonstrate a superior way of life. Through many centuries we can read records of how Christian behavior attracted pagans to Christ.

DAY 29

Being in the World But Not of the World

As in English, so in other languages: a word may have different meanings in different contexts. Think of the English words "train" (verb and noun) and "crown." The word "world" is a case in point. It can refer to the physical world that God made (Acts 17.24) or the world of people that God loves (John 3.16) or the realm of evil people and things (1 John 2.15–17). In this last text John stated that Christians are not to love that kind of world, and then he explains what "world" means here: desires of the flesh, desires of the eyes, and the pride of possessions (v 16). One translation has for that last phrase, "the boasting of what he has and does" (NIV). Those are the kinds of values and behaviors that disciples of Jesus are to avoid, because they are devoted to Him who said, "You are not of the world" (John 15.19). For this world we might think of our culture and its core values.

On the other hand, Christians are to be "in the world" of people. If not, how can they be "salt and light" as Jesus directed? (Matt 5.13–16). Jesus sent His apostles into the "world" because they were to teach it about Jesus (John 17.18). It is necessary for us to be in the world, among sinful people who care little for God; but we are not to be "of the world." Christians are to be distinguished by "marching to a different drummer."

Obedience to the command to "love not the world" is not to avoid the world but to be in it and on guard. It is dangerous to choose unholy people as your close associates. Paul quoted a known proverb on this point: "Bad company ruins good morals" (1 Cor 15.33). So, be among bad people with good purposes, but not to partake in their evil deeds—as Jesus did. Christians are not meant for the monastery but for the marketplace, not to be hermits but to be hunters for people whom they can serve in the name of Christ.

Be on guard against the potential evil influences found in various magazines, movies, various kinds of music and television. They may not be all bad, but therein lies part of the problem. Learn to discern. Be *in* the world but not *of* the world, for God.

DAY 30
Being Transformed

Some people are happy with what they are and thus are not interested in changing. That condition may be good or bad; it depends on what the person is! When one is a Christian he or she should never want to change back to the old way of life. On the other hand, the disciple of Jesus should never be entirely satisfied with the level of godliness he or she has reached. There are always bright possibilities ahead. Godliness is a huge frontier.

God determined beforehand what He wanted people to be when He sent Jesus into the world. One element of that plan was for them "to be conformed to the image of his Son" (Rom 8.29). This posture is similar to "walking in his steps" and following His example, noted earlier; but this concept is one that involves our souls, our "selves." In our thinking and feelings we are to strive to be like Jesus—appropriate for Jesus-followers. At first that seems impossible, doesn't it? We know quite well that there is a big difference between Jesus' life and the way we think and act. But wait. Something else is important here.

Paul stated that these changes within us are occurring "from one degree of glory to another" (2 Cor 3.18). It is a process. In high school—maybe even earlier—we learned in biology about "metamorphosis," the process of change in the life-cycle of an insect. Actually, biologists formed that word from the Greek word used here by Paul for "transformed." Here in 2 Corinthians 3, Paul stresses that this process is really from God through the Spirit. However, we need to be sure we cooperate, that we yield to the influence of God, of His Word, and the encouragement of fellow-Christians. Many of the things we have noticed in previous sections—the Lord's supper, singing, prayer, feeding on the Word of God—are designed to produce Christ-like character in us. God wants us to partake of His nature, the "divine nature" (2 Pet 1.4).

Partaking of God's nature, His way of behaving, is one big way in which we honor and respect Him.

DAY 31

Love, the Christian's Highest Ethic

In the New Testament there are two different words for our one English word "love." The first refers to that affection a person feels toward another person or thing that he esteems as valuable or favorable, as when one friend "loves" another or a person "loves" the world. But that is not the characteristic Christian virtue of "love." It is described and emphasized in 1 Corinthians 13.1–13. Whatever this love is, it never ends; it abides. But how does it differ from the love one has for parents, brothers and sisters, and dear friends?

First, it can be *commanded*, as when Jesus said, "Love one another" (John 13.34). We cannot "love" someone—at least in the usual sense of that word in English—who has mistreated us or harmed us, just because we are commanded to do so, can we? No matter how much we may be threatened, we just cannot love (esteem as nice, likeable) someone whose actions we find despicable. Thus, there must be something different about this kind of love. What is it? It is very important since it is the "badge" of discipleship (John 13.35).

This kind of love helps to define God (1 John 4.8). In love God reached out to the unlovely, that is, sinners. In spite of human sinfulness and rebellion God sought what was best for them. That is the reason Jesus said to "love your enemies and pray for those who persecute you." (Matt 5.43–44). He is not commanding people to *like* those who harm and persecute them; He is saying that His followers should seek what is best for those who need help. That is what God did for us, "while we were yet sinners."

This is not always easy, but it is the kind of responsible behavior the disciples of Jesus should follow. It makes a big difference in the lives of others when we do that. In many respects it takes a lifetime to develop a good practice of seeking what is best for others. It makes friends of enemies, it heals the hurting, and it repairs the damaged.

Well, you know what it means to you for God to love you! *So, do that for other humans and thus reflect the nature of your Heavenly Father (Matt 5.45).*

DAY 32
On Being a Disciple of Jesus

Jesus constantly called people to be his "disciples," and he set down the terms on which people could be his disciples. Three times in Luke 14 Jesus said that if a person did not do this or that he or she "cannot be my disciple" (vv 26, 27, 33). But what or who is a disciple? That, not the name "Christian," is what all the earliest followers of Jesus were called (see Acts 11.26). But what makes a disciple?

At the simplest level, a disciple is a "learner." But while Jesus did call people to "take my yoke upon you and learn from me" (Matt 11.29), more was involved than just being a pupil who learns principles from Jesus as a mere teacher. Repeatedly Jesus called people to "Follow me" (Matt 4.19; 8.22; Luke 9.23; John 12.26). When we were baptized we were baptized "into Christ," into a relationship with him. One of Jesus' apostles urged his readers to "follow in his steps" (1 Pet 2.21) and another to "walk as Jesus did" (1 John 2.6). It matters little at what physical age we become Christians it always involves something like little children taking their father's hand and walking confidently with him. They trust him to know the way. Similarly, we are to trust Jesus who is the way (John 14.6).

At times we sing a song that has in it these words: "Follow, follow, I will follow Jesus; anywhere, everywhere, I will follow on." That is the idea of being His disciple.

You will notice that this is very different from "being baptized into a church," as if baptism is simply the door to membership in a church. People can be members of any number of churches without being disciples of Jesus; but being baptized into Christ, committing ourselves to following Him, gives us a new dynamic by which to live, a new love and attraction. That provides us with great help to live a better life.

Today, pray for at least two things: be thankful that God has adopted you into His family. Then ask God to help you to be a good family member, loving and serving your brothers and sisters.

DAY 33
The Providence of God

The word "providence" is not found in most translations of the Bible, but the idea is written very large in both Old and New Testaments. It is found in the stories of Joseph,

Esther, Daniel and many others. Think of it as "provide-ance." God's providence does not always involve what we call miracles; often nothing spectacular is noticed. But God works in His own way to provide what is best for His people (Rom 8.28).

That does not mean that God does what we expect Him to do in every case. At times God disciplines His children for their good that they may grow stronger and "share in his holiness" (Heb 12.10). On one occasion God gave Paul what he called a "thorn in the flesh" so he would not become too excited or elated about the visions he had seen (2 Cor 12.7). Paul prayed for it to be removed but God refused. Rather, God said, "My grace is sufficient for you, for my power is made perfect in weakness" (v 9). Some of our greatest Christian hymns and books were written by people whom God had permitted to suffer set-backs and disappointments.

While Christians may have setbacks, Jesus taught that His disciples are not to worry, not to be "anxious" about the basic needs of life. He said that the God who pro-vides for birds and flowers will surely provide for *people* because they are more important than birds and flowers (read Matt 6.25–34). God provides, and He wants us to trust Him to do what He says He will do. Often we do not see what God has been doing until we look back, even over many years. How wonderful and powerful God is! How blessed we are to belong to Him!

Two other passages of Scripture assure us that we should not worry like the people who do not know God. Read Philippians 4.6–7 and 1 Peter 5.6–7. We are to cast our anxieties on God because "he cares for you." Yes, we may make our requests known to Him, and having done that we are assured that the peace of God will guard our hearts and minds. What a great promise!

Yes, we can believe in and trust the providence of God. He cares for us. "Thank you, dear God."

DAY 34

Taking Stock of Yourself

Self-evaluation is an important part of living. Schools are required to do it periodically. Businesses do it in order to be more efficient. In fact, some organizations follow a SWOT method of evaluation by identifying their **S**trengths, **W**eaknesses, **O**pportunities and **T**hreats. Jesus' servant, Paul, urged the Corinthian disciples to "examine yourselves, to see whether you are in the faith. Test yourselves" (2 Cor 13.5). They were told earlier that they should do that during the Lord's supper (1 Cor 11.28), but it may be done often and in many circumstances.

If we don't examine ourselves we are in great danger of being spiritually blind, blind to our own faults and needs. Jesus once accused the hypocritical Pharisees of being "blind guides." Three times He used the word "blind" to describe their inability to see their own faults (Matt 23.16–22). It is a very healthy thing to examine ourselves to see how well we are progressing.

At this point you have been a Christian for a month or more. How are you getting along? Take pen and paper and respond to the following items, *just for you*:

1. What are some of the things about which you feel good as a Christian?

2. What have you learned about being a Christian that particularly pleases you and makes you happy?

3. Is anything discouraging to you at the moment?

4. What things about the Christian life raise questions in your mind?

5. If you are having any problems as a Christian, what are they?

Now, what can you do with this list?

First, *you can pray about any of those things about which you need to speak to God.* *Second*, *if you have by now a trusted Christian friend, you may wish to speak to him or her about these items.*

Remember, Christians are to help "each other."

DAY 35

Devote Your Speech to God (1)

Scripture teaches us what we might learn from observation: "The tongue has the power of life and death" (Prov 18.21). People have been sent to prison, or even killed, because someone lied about them. On the other hand, people have become Christians, been saved from a life of sin, or spurred on to loyalty, because someone used her or his "tongue" in a constructive manner. Christians, children of God, are to use their speech constructively and helpfully.

A part of the new life in Christ is this: "Do not lie to each other" (Col 3.9). Each of us is to "put off falsehood and speak truthfully to his neighbor" (Eph 4.25). Jesus-followers are not to lie to anyone, including themselves. Read James 3.1–12 and note the importance of controlling the tongue. Much harm can be done when we falsify to family, friends, and brothers and sisters in Christ. Our Master, Jesus, said, "Simply let your 'Yes' be 'Yes,' and your 'No,' 'No'" (Matt 5.33–37). Be honest. You need not tell all you know; just be truthful when you speak.

Some people develop early in life the habit of lying to maintain relationships and protect themselves from harm. That is a big mistake on several counts. It is unlike our Heavenly Father, who does not lie (Heb 6.18). Second, it is not a realistic way of carrying on life since one who lies must always look over her or his shoulder to see whether someone has discovered the lies that were told. Further, it is often difficult to remember what was said if the truth was not told. Finally, it can be a hard habit to break. Many people in their 40s and 50s still struggle with the practice of falsifying which they developed earlier in life. Break it!

But God will help all of us when we seek His help by prayer and diligent effort. Was it Abraham Lincoln who said, "Honesty is the best policy?" It may be, but honesty is chiefly a virtue because it is the Christian way of life. It is Godlike. What a disaster it would be were God and Jesus untruthful with us!

Pray: "Dear Lord, You always tell us the truth. Help me to be like You in that regard. In Jesus' name. Amen."

DAY 36
Devote Your Speech to God (2)

Now let us focus more on the positive aspects of our speech, of using our tongues for constructive, wholesome, righteous purposes. This is a vast and important subject in Scripture. The little book of James mentions in each of its five chapters something about proper speech; the book of Proverbs is full of instructions about good and bad speech activities.

In Proverbs alone we learn that speech can be used to nourish/feed (10.21), heal (12.18; 16.24), cheer (12.25), instruct/persuade for good (16.21), bring good news (25.25), and give faithful instruction (31.26). In the New Testament we are informed that our speech can encourage (Heb 10.25; 1 Thes 4.18; 5.11), sympathize and comfort (1 Cor 14.3), and build up (1 Cor 14.26). Give some thought to the ways in which you can use your speech when your friends are discouraged, sorrowing due to the loss of a loved one, or worriying about some situation. At times it is appropriate to write your words in a card or letter. Many people, even strangers, have been lifted up because Christians cheered them with appropriate speech.

One never knows what the outcome will be when his or her speech is used to invite someone to a Christian activity: a fellowship, a Bible study, a social gathering.

Andrew heard John the Baptist preaching and began to follow him. Then he found his brother, whom we know as Peter, and spoke to him about the Messiah (John 1.40–42). We read little about Andrew after that, but we read a lot about what Peter became! You never know what will happen when you use your speech to introduce someone to Jesus or to encourage someone who is faltering. In the future what use might God make of your speech? God can bring great good from small events. Do all you can to develop this gift from God. It might be one of your big ministries for the Lord.

Pray: "O Lord, please help me to grow in my ability to speak for You, to use my tongue for your glory. In Jesus' name. Amen.

Day 37

Revelation: Is Your Faith Merely a Matter of Preference?

In our country, as in other places, many people regard religion as mere preference, like one's taste for music or graphic art. To them, truth is a very slippery and uncertain entity! "Truth is what is truth to you," they say. When Jesus was on trial before him, Pilate cynically asked, "What is truth?" (John 18.38). Is your faith as a Christian based on mere guesswork, mere human opinion and preference? Not at all.

Scripture claims to be "inspired of God," or "God breathed" (2 Tim 3.16–17). Before the time of Jesus, the prophets did not speak out of their human perceptions of events. Rather they "spoke from God as they were carried along by the Holy Spirit" (2 Pet 1.21). There are many evidences that make these claims true. This means that Scripture is a God-guided account of what has happened in the past and what God wants people to do now. When we are able to verify statements in Scripture by archeology and ancient texts we find that it is a book that deal with truth, not illusion or mere fancy. Entire books have been written on the truthfulness and trustworthiness of Scripture.

The content of the gospel message—the life and teachings of Jesus, his death, burial and resurrection and their meanings—were not inventions of men and women. Paul was quite clear about the fact that what he taught was not a product of man but "a revelation [uncovering, laying bare] from Jesus Christ" (Gal 1.11–12). God acted in decisive and dramatic ways to declare the identity of Jesus as the Son of God, including raising him from the dead (Rom 1.4). When Jesus' apostles explained the meaning and significance of his death, burial and resurrection, the Holy Spirit authenticated that message by signs and wonders of an extraordinary nature (Acts 14.3; 15.8, 12; Heb 2.1–4).

Jesus' apostles (that is, His envoys) were not self-appointed; Jesus selected and trained them. Paul pointed out that the true apostles, in contrast to the false apostles at Corinth, bore the signs of an apostle (2 Cor 12.12).

The information we have about God, Jesus, and the Holy Spirit bears the marks of authenticity. Paul would not have made up such a system and stuck with it since it caused him so much grief. No. *Our belief as followers of Jesus is a product of revelation from God. We are not guessing!*

DAY 38

Strangers and Exiles in the Earth

It is likely that none of us has ever been an exile. History records how many people in Africa, Europe, and the Middle East who have fled harsh dictators or war conditions in their home countries to become exiles in other countries. But most of us have had no such experiences. Exiles, strangers, sojourners are those who are citizens of one country but are living (usually temporarily) in another, whether forced or choosing to do so. When the Jews were taken away into Babylonian captivity, Jeremiah wrote them a letter from Jerusalem, giving a message from God. "Build houses and live in them; plant gardens" and so forth. "Seek the welfare of the city where I have sent you into exile." You will be there for 70 years, as I told you, but you have a future. You will return to your homeland (Jer 29.4–14).

A New Testament writer pointed out that the faithful Jews of the past were "strangers and exiles in the earth" (Heb 11.13) because God was their focus. Some translations use words like "sojourners" and "pilgrims" to translate the Greek words here rendered "exiles." You get the idea.

Peter declared that Christians, simply because they are Christians, are "strangers and exiles" and should behave among non-Christians in such a way that they will glorify God (2 Pet 2.11–12).

Paul did not use terms like "strangers" and "exiles," but

he explained why Christians are at least sojourners on the earth: "our citizenship is in heaven" (Phil 3.20–21). Heaven is headquarters; that is the seat of the commonwealth. We are temporarily on earth.

What does this mean for life? Among other things, we should learn to long for "home." That will develop for you in time. This realm, called "the world," should not determine our values and norms. Yes, we find ourselves doing what non-Christians do in having jobs, marrying, taking vacations (retreats from the tedium of life), and so forth. But as Jesus-followers we do some of the same things *with different motives*. This realm will pass away, but "whoever does the will of God abides forever" (1 John 2.15–17). *We are to live and serve in this world but with a consciousness that we belong to another realm.* That is a part of the Christian world-view and keeps us in balance. We are not to live in monasteries but among people so we can be salt and light. We have employment, families, friends, and even recreational activities; but their relative values change as we become more and more what God wants us to be in heart. Our motives are different. Both actions and motives are to be rooted in God's intentions for us as His people.

Today pray that God will strengthen you in the development of your distinctive Christian identity, strengthen you as you seek to develop a responsible, informed Christian world-view.

DAY 39

Jesus: Our High Priest and Intercessor

In the church that Jesus started through his apostles there was no separate class of people who were called priests. However, like the nation of Israel (Exod 19.6), the whole church of Christ is said to be a "royal priesthood" (1 Pet 2.9) in the sense that all its members have access to God and have a mission in the world of bringing the pagans to God. However, Christians have a *high priest*, Jesus.

One reason for Jesus' coming in the flesh was to identify with humans. Having done so, suffering and being tempted in this world, He can be a "merciful and faithful high priest" on behalf of us humans (Heb 2.14–18). He can speak to God for us. From the Gospels we learn that He grew tired and thirsty. He knew what human pain was, having suffered severely both before and during His crucifixion. It is reassuring to know that the high priest who represents us to God is one who has lived in our kind of world and been tempted.

Although Jesus was the Son of God, He "became flesh" (John 1.14) and lived in our kind of world. Thus, it is said that He is "able to sympathize with our weaknesses" when He acts as our high priest. Therefore, we should be confident (Heb 4.15–16).

Jesus offered Himself as a sinless sacrifice for us (Heb 9.14). On that basis He is now in heaven "to appear in the presence of God on our behalf" (Heb 9.24). What an astounding benefit that is!

Earlier we considered what Christians should do about their sins. But here we note another of the provisions God has made for our forgiveness, growth, and development. Jesus stands in the presence of God *for us, on our behalf.* That is a very reassuring benefit of being a child of God. We are not alone. God is for us. He wants us to be saved from both the *guilt* of sins and the *practice* of sinning. Sin is no more to be the norm for us; it is to be the exception in our behavior.

Thank God for providing for us a great High Priest.

DAY 40

Going on to Maturity

Jesse Bankhead, a friend of mine, had an acquaintance named Cephas who would play with his dolls and stand at the window and look at the cows. There was nothing wrong with that, except that Cephas was 74 years old and wore diapers. He had failed to develop. That is very sad when it is an unwanted and uncontrollable physical condition. But what if it is a chosen spiritual condition?

These lessons have been designed to point out some of the steps new Christians need to take in order to climb up to higher ground. In one of our hymns we sing, "I'm pressing on the upward way, new heights I'm gaining every day." That is what God wants to help us do. He will do much more in the process than we will do, but it still requires our effort, our yielding to His molding activity in our lives. We are not passive in the situation, as if God zaps us with spiritual lightning. That is the reason we often read directives such as "Put off all of these," "Seek those things that are above," "think about these things," and so forth. The writer of the book of Hebrews was addressing believers who were backing off because they were experiencing some degree if persecution (12.3–11). Among the things he urged them to do was to "leave the elementary teachings about Christ and go on to maturity" (Heb 6.1). In the previous chapter he rebuked them for their failure to develop, for remaining infants who needed to drink milk! He then noted that the mature can eat solid food because "they have trained themselves to distinguish good from evil" (5.12–14).

Having gone through these little exercises for 40 days, make it your aim, set it as an ongoing goal, to *press on to maturity*. You have now learned, if only at an introductory level, many things God has provided for you as a new Christian. Determine to use them for their intended purposes. If you will, then God will make you "an instrument for noble purposes, made holy, useful to the Master and prepared to do any good work" (2 Tim 2.20–21).

Walk with him and your path will end in heaven!

Among the Risen!

Risen! Yes, you are among the risen. When Jesus died on the cross He was a sin-offering for us; He bore our sins in His body (1 Pet 2.24; Heb 9.24). Additionally, His resurrection from the dead involves our deliverance. Jesus' resurrection was described in all four Gospels and was at the heart of early Christian preaching (1 Cor 15.1–4), but few of us realize everything that was involved in that resurrection. Jesus rose to die no more (Rom 6.9); He conquered death as a human experience. His resurrection is the guarantee that all who have died will be resurrected eventually (1 Cor 15.20–25). Some will be resurrected to life and other to judgment (John 5.28–9), but human physical death will have ended. "The last enemy to be destroyed is death" (v 26). Through the resurrection of Jesus God triumphed over evil forces largely unknown to us (Col 2.14–15).

What does this mean to you? First, you are involved in it. When your trust in Jesus expressed itself in your baptism "into Christ" you were identified with His death, burial, and resurrection. You were baptized "into his death" (Rom 6.1–4). You identified with His death in that your repentance meant that you had decided in your heart to turn from sin, turn from your former way of life, and live for God. As Paul wrote, your "old self was crucified with him that the body of sin might be brought to nothing" (v 6). Then, you were identified with His resurrection. When you were raised up from baptism you were raised to "walk in newness of life" (Rom 6.4). The Christians at Ephesus were reminded that, whereas they had been "dead in trespasses and sins" they had been "made alive together with Christ ... and raised up" to a new realm of life (Eph 2.1, 5). The apostle Paul stated it pointedly to the church in Colossae: you have been "buried with him in baptism, in which you were also raised with him through faith in the powerful working of God, who raised him from the dead. And you, who were dead in your trespasses ... God made alive together with him ..." (Col 2.12–13). So, just as it was wonderful, incredibly good news that "He is risen!" (Matt 28.6–7; Mark 16.16), it is wonderful to know that when we become Christians, we are raised with Him. We are among the risen!

Now what? Scripture teaches that we are raised to "walk in newness of life" (Rom 6.4; 2 Cor 5.17; Eph 4.22–24; Col 3.10). Being "raised with Christ" is not the end of a spiritual journey; it is the beginning of a new journey with a new dynamic by which to live. This little booklet is designed to help you with a good start on that journey. Happy travels!

Bulk Rate Prices for *Risen!*

1–9	Full price
10–24	10% discount
25–49	20% discount
50–99	30% discount
100+	40% discount

For a full listing of DeWard Publishing Company books, visit our website:

www.deward.com

CPSIA information can be obtained
at www.ICGtesting.com
Printed in the USA
FSHW011503250821
84306FS